Communities

Living in a
City

by Lisa Trumbauer

Consulting Editor: Gail Saunders-Smith, PhD

Capstone
press

Mankato, Minnesota

Pebble Books are published by Capstone Press,
151 Good Counsel Drive, P.O. Box 669, Mankato, Minnesota 56002.
www.capstonepress.com

1 2 3 4 5 6 10 09 08 07 06 05

Library of Congress Cataloging-in-Publication Data
Trumbauer, Lisa, 1963–
   Living in a city / by Lisa Trumbauer.
   p. cm.—(Communities)
   Includes bibliographical references and index.
   ISBN 0-7368-3630-6 (hardcover)
   1. Cities and towns—Juvenile literature. 2. City and town life—Juvenile
literature. I. Title. II. Series.
HT119.T78 2005
307.76—dc22   2004009601

Summary: Simple text and photographs describe life in a city.

Note to Parents and Teachers

The Communities set supports social studies standards related to
people, places, and geography. This book describes and illustrates
cities. The images support early readers in understanding the text.
The repetition of words and phrases helps early readers learn new
words. This book also introduces early readers to subject-specific
vocabulary words, which are defined in the Glossary section. Early
readers may need assistance to read some words and to use the
Table of Contents, Glossary, Read More, Internet Sites, and Index
sections of the book.

Table of Contents

Cities 5
Work and School 11
Fun in a City 17

Glossary 22
Read More 23
Internet Sites 23
Index 24

Cities

A city is a
big community.
Many people live
and work in a city.
Cities can be crowded.

Each neighborhood
in a city is different.
People live and work
in neighborhoods.

Most people in cities
live in apartments
or houses.

Work and School

In a city, many people
work in tall buildings.
The tallest buildings
are called skyscrapers.

A city has busy streets
with noisy traffic.
People ride in cars, buses,
and taxis to get to work.

A city has many
schools and colleges.
Students learn
at schools and colleges.

Fun in a City

People play in city parks.
People also have fun
shopping at stores
in cities. They go
out to eat.

A city has theaters.
People listen to music
and watch plays
in theaters.

Every state has
at least one big city.
Do you live in a city?

Glossary

college—a school where people go to study after high school

community—a group of people who live in the same area

neighborhood—a small area within a city where people live

skyscraper—a very tall building

theater—a place where movies, plays, or concerts are shown or performed

traffic—moving vehicles; traffic includes cars, taxis, buses, trucks, and bicycles.

Read More

Holland, Gini. *I Live in the City.* Where I Live. Milwaukee: Weekly Reader Early Learning Library, 2004.

Jacobs, Daniel. *City Shapes.* Bloomington, Minn.: Yellow Umbrella Books, 2004.

Scheunemann, Pam. *Cities.* Capital Letters. Edina, Minn.: Abdo, 2001.

Internet Sites

FactHound offers a safe, fun way to find Internet sites related to this book. All of the sites on FactHound have been researched by our staff.

Here's how:

1. Visit *www.facthound.com*

2. Type in this special code **0736836306** for age-appropriate sites. Or enter a search word related to this book for a more general search.

3. Click on the **Fetch It** button.

FactHound will fetch the best sites for you!

Index

apartments, 9
buses, 13
cars, 13
colleges, 15
community, 5
crowded, 5
houses, 9
music, 19
neighborhoods, 7
noisy, 13
parks, 17

plays, 19
schools, 15
shopping, 17
skyscrapers, 11
state, 21
stores, 17
streets, 13
taxis, 13
theaters, 19
traffic, 13
work, 5, 7, 11, 13

Word Count: 133
Grade: 1
Early-Intervention Level: 13

Editorial Credits

Mari C. Schuh, editor; Kate Opseth, designer; Jo Miller, photo researcher; Scott Thoms, photo editor

Photo Credits

Bruce Coleman Inc./Joan Iaconetti, 6; Bruce Coleman Inc./Phil Degginger, 4; Capstone Press/Karon Dubke, 8; Digital Stock, 1; Digital Vision, cover (boy); Doranne Jacobson, 20 Folio, Inc./Everett C. Johnson, 14; The Image Finders/Jim Baron, 16; Image Ideas Inc., cover (background); Patrick Batchelder, 12; Photodisc, 10; Richard Hamilton Smith, 18